Marriage

Spencer W. Kimball

Marriage

Deseret Book Company
Salt Lake City, Utah
1981

Library of Congress Cataloging in Publication Data

Kimball, Spencer W., 1895-
  Marriage.

  CONTENTS: John and Mary, beginning
life together.—Marriage and divorce.
  1. Marriage. 2. Divorce. 3. Mormons and
mormonism. I. Kimball, Spencer W., 1895-
Marriage and divorce. 1978. II. Title.
HQ734.K4818   261.8′34′2   78-4132
ISBN 0-87747-675-6

John
and Mary,
beginning
life
together

Across the desk from me sits a delightful young couple. They have come to ask me to perform the marriage ceremony for them in the temple of the Lord. The young man has penetrating eyes, curly hair, and a captivating smile. The young woman is alert and lovely, her dark hair adding glory to her shining face, which she frequently lifts up to her companion in adoration. Here is the love of youth at its best and sweetest. And when they are comfortably seated near one another so that their hands are sometimes touching, I say to them:

And so you are going to be married, John and Mary! And tomorrow is the great day!

How happy I am for you as you approach this sacred hour! Congratulations to you, John and Mary, and I wish for you eternities of happiness. This you want —this you may have—if you will do the things of which I tell you here today.

Happiness, though, is an elusive thing, John and Mary. It is a little like the pot of gold at the end of the rainbow. If you go out deliberately to find it, you may have great difficulty catching it. But if you will follow directions closely, you will not need to pursue it. It will overtake you and remain with you.

Happiness is a strange commodity. It cannot be purchased with money, and yet it is bought with a price. It is not dependent upon houses, or lands, or flocks, or degrees, or position, or comforts, for many of the most unhappy people in all the world have these. The millionaire has comforts and luxuries, but he has no happiness unless he has paid the same price for it that you can also pay. Often the rich are the most unhappy.

If you think that ease and comfort and money are necessary to your happiness, ask your parents and others whose lives are in the autumn. If they have been financially successful, they will generally tell you that the happiest days were not the ones when they were retired, with a palatial home, two cars in the garage, and money with which to travel around the world; but their joyous days were those when they, too, planned and worked for the wherewithal to make ends meet; when they had their little ones about them and were wholly absorbed in family life and church work.

And so, Mary and John, you may live

*A simple, quiet, but beautiful marriage in the temple,
a sweet eternal ceremony that will be
unostentatious and sacred like your birth,
blessing, baptism, or ordination.*

in a single room or a small cabin and be happy. You may ride the bus or walk instead of riding in a luxurious car, and still be happy. You may wear your clothes more than a single season and still be happy.

You ask, "What is the price of happiness?" You will be surprised at the simplicity of the answer. The treasure house of happiness may be unlocked and remain open to those who use the following keys. First, you must live the gospel of Jesus Christ in its purity and simplicity—not a half-hearted compliance, but hewing to the line, and this means an all-out devoted consecration to the great program of salvation and exaltation in an orthodox manner. Second, you must forget yourself and love your companion more than yourself. If you do these things, happiness will be yours in great and never-failing abundance.

Now, the living of the gospel is not a thing of the letter, but of the spirit, and your attitudes toward it are far more important than the mechanics of it, but a combination of doing and feeling will bring spiritual, mental, and temporal advancement and growth.

Mary and John, I congratulate you for

your vision and faith and your willingness to forgo the fanfare and glamour of a worldly wedding for a simple, quiet, but beautiful marriage in the temple, a sweet eternal ceremony that will be unostentatious and sacred like your birth, blessing, baptism, or ordination.

Because your people are prosperous, Mary, I realize you could have had all that the world might offer in a glamorous wedding with candles and flowers, attendants and pageantry. But you chose the simple, sacred way—the Lord's way. I salute you!

You could have been married on a merry-go-round as a couple recently were on television, exchanging vows astride painted wooden horses, for which they were to receive all expenses for a wedding trip. You, Mary and John, would not be willing to commercialize on this sacred ordinance and sell your "birthright for a mess of pottage." You are like many other devoted Latter-day Saint people who prefer to be married in the house of the Lord. John and Mary, I commend you.

I know you plan a reception following the marriage. It offers a delightful opportunity for relatives and friends to bring gifts and wish you well, but I hope you will again avoid temptation to go to extremes in following the world in showy pageantry. There is danger that the ostentatious display may detract from and overshadow the simple wedding. With your good judgment and clear thinking, I know you can graciously entertain your guests at a wholesome, friendly, and dignified reception without the excesses so often in evidence.

Now, Mary, you must understand that John will not be able to support you as has your father, who has been accumulating for a quarter century; John is just starting. For that matter, perhaps he never will have as much as your father.

And furthermore, Mary, with your wholesome attitude toward family life, I know you will desire to devote your life to your home and family, so when you resign your job and no longer have that income to spend upon yourself, it will mean many adjustments for you; but I understand you have considered all those things and are willing. You see, Mary, it was never intended by the Lord that married women should compete with men in employment. They have a far greater and more important service to render, and so you give up your employment and settle down to become the queen of the little new home that you will proceed to transform into a heaven for John, this man whom you adore. John will work hard and will do his best to provide you with comforts and even luxuries later, but this is the perfect way, to "start from scratch" together.

And, Mary, you have much to learn in these coming months. Perhaps you, like most of the other young women of the nation, have prepared yourself for a career that you will not follow. One college president said about ninety-two percent of all the girls in his college studied languages and mathematics and business; and then when they were married they found that they not only had limited use for their specialized training, but they had also failed to train for the great career to which they were now to dedicate their lives. Mary, you are to become a career woman in the greatest career on earth—that of homemaker, wife, and mother. And so, if you failed to prepare for motherhood and homemaking when you could, you may make up somewhat by devoting yourself to those subjects now. In your spare time you could now study child psychology and

Your love, like a flower, must be nourished. There will come a great
love and interdependence between you,
for your love is a divine one.
It is deep, inclusive, comprehensive.

child discipline, the fundamentals of nursing, the art of teaching, particularly how to tell stories and teach children; and you will want to get all the theory as well as the practice now in cooking, sewing, budgeting, and buying.

John's limited income will spread far if you can learn to buy efficiently and cook expertly so that there will never be waste. And his small income can go far if you learn to make some of your own clothes and those of the children and utilize scraps and pick up bargains. And if you learn the rudiments of nursing, you may be able to save much in doctor and hospital costs by recognizing symptoms and treating minor afflictions, and you may also have the satisfaction of even saving the lives of your own precious family by your being able to do practical nursing. And so your economies will largely make up for the loss of your own income.

You wouldn't want to work outside the home anyway, Mary, for women are expected to earn the living only in emergencies, and you must know that many are the broken homes resulting when women leave their posts at home. You see, if both husband and wife are working away from home and come home tired, it is very easy for unpleasantness and misunderstandings to arise. And so, Mary, you will remain at home, making it attractive and heavenly, and when John comes home tired, you will be fresh and pleasant; the house will be orderly; the dinner will be tempting; and life will have real meaning.

And you must remember, John, that Mary's life is not always an easy one. Those months of waiting for the babies are trying ones, often associated with physical discomforts and many deprivations. You will need to be more solicitous of her comfort and more understanding if she should sometimes be irritable. You should assist her about the home and with the little ones and spend no time away from the home and family except to fulfill needed obligations imposed by church service and your occupation. You will limit your social life as she must, and to those activities in which Mary may join you.

Now, John and Mary, there may be a temptation to economize by living with the parents on either side. Do not make this serious error. You two will constitute a new family tomorrow. Well-meaning relatives have broken up many a home.

Numerous divorces are attributable to the interference of parents who thought they were only protecting their loved children. Live in your own home even though it be but a modest cottage or a tent. Live your own life. Mary, you must not go home to your parents for long visits, leaving John home alone; neither will you, John, leave Mary when it can be avoided.

And John, you will, of course, do your best to provide the home and the living. But you will not take two or three jobs in order to give Mary luxuries, for Mary has already made her mental adjustments and is willing to get along on what you can reasonably produce. And you will secure employment that is compatible with good family life, John. You will not take a traveling job that will take you away from your home, except in emergencies. Both you and Mary will prefer to have a smaller salary with you at home, rather than to have greater luxuries with you away. And if your work moves you permanently to another location, Mary will go with you, even though it means being away from family and friends, and even in less desirable places and with fewer opportunities. You are being married for that reason

—that you may always be together.

Your love, like a flower, must be nourished. There will come a great love and interdependence between you, for your love is a divine one. It is deep, inclusive, comprehensive. It is not like that association of the world which is misnamed love, but which is mostly physical attraction. When marriage is based on this only, the parties soon tire of one another. There is a break and a divorce, and a new, fresher physical attraction comes with another marriage, which in turn may last only until it too becomes stale. The love of which the Lord speaks is not only physical attraction, but spiritual attraction as well. It is faith and confidence in, and understanding of, one another. It is a total partnership. It is companionship with common ideals and standards. It is unselfishness toward and sacrifice for one another. It is cleanliness of thought and action and faith in God and his program. It is parenthood in mortality ever looking toward godhood and creationship, and parenthood of spirits. It is vast, all-inclusive, and limitless. This kind of love never tires or wanes. It lives on through sickness and sorrow, through prosperity

*Suppose an injury has been inflicted; unkind words have been said;
hearts are torn; and each feels that the
other is wholly at fault. Nothing is done to heal the wound.
The hours pass. There is a throbbing
of hearts through the night, a day of sullenness and unkindness
and further misunderstanding. Injury is
heaped upon injury until the attorney is employed,
the home broken,
and the lives of parents and children blasted.*

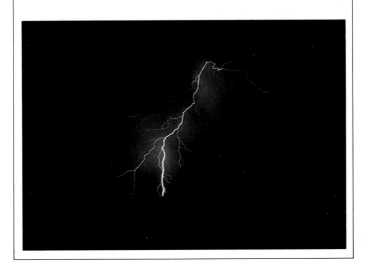

and privation, through accomplishment and disappointment, through time and eternity.

John and Mary, this is the kind of love that I feel you are bringing to one another, but even this richer, more abundant love will wilt and die if it is not given food, so you must live and treat each other in a manner that your love will grow. Today it is demonstrative love, but in the tomorrows of ten, thirty, fifty years, it will be a far greater and more intensified love, grown quieter and more dignified with the years of sacrifice, suffering, joys, and consecration to one another, to your family, and to the kingdom of God.

For your love to ripen so gloriously, there must be an increase of confidence and understanding, a frequent and sincere expression of appreciation of one another. There must be a forgetting of self and a constant concern for the other. There must be a focusing of interests and hopes and objectives into a single channel.

Now, John and Mary, many young people plan to postpone their spiritual life, church activity, and the bearing of a family until they complete their degrees or become established financially; and by the time they are prepared according to their ambitious standards, they have lost much of the inclination and powers and time.

You, John, are the head of the family. You hold the priesthood. Give this little family righteous leadership. Tomorrow at the end of your first perfect day of marriage, you two should kneel at your bedside before retiring, in your first family prayer, and thank the Lord for the love that has brought you together and for all your rich blessings, and ask him to help you to remain true to your covenants and keep clean and worthy and active. Then never let a day pass without your morning and evening devotion. Now is the time to chart your life's course. Determine to attend your priesthood and sacrament meetings every Sabbath, pay your tithing faithfully, sustain in very deed the authorities of the Church, support the programs of the Church, visit the temple often, give service in the organizations, and keep your actions constructive, your attitudes wholesome.

And, John and Mary, tomorrow when I repeat the phrases that will bind you for eternity, I shall say the same impressive words that the Lord said to that handsome youth and his lovely bride in the Garden of Eden: "Be fruitful, and multiply and replenish the earth." The Lord does not waste words. He meant what he said. You did not come on earth just to "eat, drink, and be merry." You came knowing full well your responsibilities. You came to get for yourself a mortal body that could become perfected, immortalized, and you understood that you were to act in partnership with God in providing bodies for other spirits equally anxious to come to earth for righteous purposes. And so you will not postpone parenthood. There will be rationalists who will name to you numerous reasons for postponement. Of course, it will be harder to get your college degrees or your financial start with a family, but strength like yours will be undaunted in the face of difficult obstacles. Have your family as the Lord intended. Of course it is expensive, but you will find a way, and besides, it is often those children who grow up with responsibility and hardships who carry on the world's work.

John and Mary, do not limit your family as the world does. I am wondering now where I might have been had my parents decided arbitrarily that one or two children would be enough, or that three or four would be all they could support, or that even five would be the limit; for I was the sixth of eleven children. Don't think you will love the later ones less or have fewer material things for them. Perhaps, like Jacob, you might love the eleventh one most. Young people, have your family, love them, sacrifice for them, teach them righteousness, and you will be blessed and happy all the days of your eternal lives.

Now, Mary and John, there is an indispensable element in this happiness you desire. There must be fidelity and confidence. John, you have had a legitimate and proper opportunity these past years to look the world over for a wife, to date numerous girls, and to compare and contrast them with one another, weighing their virtues and attractions; and finally, of them all you have selected Mary as the one with whom you wish to be associated forever, the one who reaches such heights of perfection in your eyes that she is worthy not only to be your helpmeet but also the mother of your posterity. You have built for Mary a pedestal, and placing her on it, you will never permit any other ever to share the place with her. She is your queen, your counterpart, your love throughout the eternities.

And you, Mary, have had the same privilege of comparing all the boys who came to see you, and you have selected John as the finest specimen of young manhood, the most desirable companion, to be your husband and the father of your children; and now, having made your choice, this is final. You have built a pedestal on which you have placed John, and no one may ever share that place with him. Never again will you look upon any man as you have John, for he is now your mate and sweetheart and husband for eternities.

Henceforth, your eyes will never wander; your thoughts will never stray; in a very literal way you will keep yourselves for each other only, in mind and body and spirit. You will remember that the Lord Jesus Christ said: "Ye have heard that it was said by them of old time, Thou shalt not commit adultery: But I say unto you, That whosoever looketh on a woman to lust after her hath committed adultery with her already in his heart." (Matthew 5:27-28.)

And it can be paraphrased also to say:

". . . she that looketh upon a man to lust after him hath committed adultery already with him in her heart." And I want to say to you also, that flirting by married people, even though they think it innocent and limited, is a serious sin and is the approach toward eventual downfall. A very large share of all divorces have their origin in infidelity of one or both parties, so you can see how important it is to heed this warning and strictly avoid even the appearance of or approach toward evil.

Now, John and Mary, being human, you may someday have differences of opinion resulting even in little quarrels. Neither of you will be so unfaithful to the other as to go back to your parents or friends and discuss with them your little differences. That would be gross disloyalty. Your intimate life is your own and must not be shared with or confided in others. You will not go back to your people for sympathy, but will thresh out your own difficulties. Suppose an injury has been inflicted; unkind words have been said; hearts are torn; and each feels that the other is wholly at fault. Nothing is done to heal the wound. The hours pass. There is a throbbing of hearts through the night, a day of sullenness and unkindness and further misunderstanding. Injury is heaped upon injury until the attorney is employed, the home broken, and the lives of parents and children blasted.

But there is a healing balm which, if applied early, in but a few minutes will return you to sane thinking; and know that, with so much at stake—your love, yourselves, your family, your ideals, your exaltation, your eternities—you cannot afford to take chances. You must swallow your pride and with courage, you, John, would say: "Mary, darling, I'm sorry. I didn't mean to hurt you. Please forgive me." And Mary, you would reply: "John, dear, it was I who was at fault more than you. Please forgive me." And you go into one another's arms and life is on an even keel again. And when you retire at night, it is forgotten, and there is no chasm between you as you have your family prayer. This time you could thank the Lord for the courage and strength he helped you muster to avert a threatened calamity. And with this fortitude and determination, you will find that the misunderstandings will reduce in numbers, and whereas they may have come at intervals of weeks, the intervals will come to be months and years, and finally you will learn wholly to enmesh your lives, forever barring the pettiness that is so disastrous.

Now, tomorrow is the glorious and eventful day. I'll meet you at the temple in the beautiful room decorated in white, typifying purity. The walls of the temple will shut out the sounds of the world below. There in sweet composure the ceremony will be performed to unite you two for all eternity. Your immediate family and closest friends will be there and with you will rise to spiritual heights in this heaven upon earth.

And when the ceremony is completed, you two will go forth from those sacred precincts, your thoughts on a high spiritual plane a "little lower than the angels." Hand in hand, with your eyes to the light, you will go forth to conquer and build and love and exalt yourselves and your family.

Goodbye until tomorrow, my beloved John and Mary, and God bless you always.

Marriage
and
Divorce

Through the years I have warned the youth of Zion against the sins and vices so prevalent in our society—those of sexual impurity and all of its many ugly approaches. I have spoken of immodesty in dress and actions as one of the softening processes of Lucifer.

I have spoken plainly, warning youth of the pitfalls of petting and of all the other perversions into which young men and young women sometimes fall. I have endeavored also to give hope to those who might have stepped over the bounds of propriety, and I have outlined to them the path by which total repentance might bring them to forgiveness.

I have warned the youth against the many hazards of interfaith marriage, and with all the power I possess, I have warned young people to avoid the sorrows and disillusionments that come from marrying out of the Church and the unhappy situations that almost invariably result when a believer marries an unbelieving spouse. I have pointed out the demands of the Church upon its members in time, energy, and funds; the deepness of the spiritual ties that tighten after marriage and as the family comes; the antagonisms that naturally follow such mismating; and that these and many other reasons argue eloquently for marriage within the Church where husband and wife have common backgrounds, common ideals and standards, common beliefs, hopes, and objectives, and above all, where marriage may be eternalized through righteous entry into the holy temple.

Now I wish to follow these important principles with a discussion of family life. This topic is not new nor is it spectacular, but it is vital. Marriage is relevant in every life, and family life is the basis of our existence. I make no apology for discussing this subject. Like Paul, I am pressed in the spirit to warn and to strengthen. May I have the blessings of our Heavenly Father in my words.

The ugly dragon of divorce has entered into our social life. Little known to our grandparents and not even common among our parents, this cancer has come to be so common in our own day that nearly every family has been cursed by its destructive machinations. This is one of the principal tools of Satan to destroy faith, through breaking up happy homes and bringing frustration of life and distortion of thought.

Honorable, happy, and successful marriage is surely the principal goal of every normal person. One who would purposely or neglectfully avoid its serious implications is not only not normal, but is frustrating his own program. There are also a few people who marry for spite or marry for wealth or marry on the rebound after having been jilted. How distorted is the thinking of such a one!

Marriage is perhaps the most vital of all the decisions and has the most far-reaching effects, for it has to do not only with immediate happiness, but eternal joys as well. It affects not only the two people involved, but also their families and particularly their children and their children's children down through the many generations. It is absolutely appalling how many children today are growing up in our society who do not have two parents, a father and a mother—and neither one is totally sufficient, if two could be had.

In selecting a companion for life and for eternity, certainly the most careful planning and thinking and praying and fasting should be done to be sure that of all the decisions, this one must not be wrong. In true marriage there must be a union of minds as well as of hearts. Emotions must not wholly determine decisions, but the mind and the heart, strengthened by fasting and prayer and serious consideration, will give one a maximum chance of marital happiness.

Marriage is not easy; it is not simple, as evidenced by the ever-mounting divorce rate. Exact figures astound us. The following ones come from Salt Lake County, which are probably somewhere near average. There were 832 marriages in a single month, and there were 414 divorces. That is half as many divorces as marriages. There were 364 temple marriages and of the temple marriages, about 10 percent were dissolved by divorce. This is substantially better than the average, but we are chagrined that there should be *any* divorce following a temple marriage.

We are grateful that this one survey reveals that about 90 percent of the temple marriages hold fast. Because of this, we recommend that people marry those who are of the same racial background generally, and of somewhat the same economic and social and educational background. Some of these are not an absolute necessity, but preferred; and above all, the same religious background, without question. In spite of the most favorable matings, the evil one still takes a monumental toll and is the cause for many broken homes and frustrated lives.

With all conditions as nearly ideal as possible, there are still people who terminate their marriages for the reason of "incompatibility." We see so many movies and television programs and read so much fiction and come in contact with so many society scandals that the people in general come to think of "marrying and giving in marriage," divorcing and remarrying, as the normal patterns.

The divorce itself does not constitute the entire evil, but the very acceptance of divorce as a cure is also a serious sin of this generation. Because a program or a pattern is universally accepted is not evidence that it is right. Marriage never was easy. It may never be. It brings with it sacrifice, sharing, and a demand for great selflessness.

Many of the TV and movie screen shows and stories of fiction end with marriage, and "they lived happily ever after."

*In true marriage there must be a union of
minds as well as of hearts. Emotions must not wholly
determine decisions, but the mind and the heart, strengthened by
fasting and prayer and serious
consideration, will give one a maximum chance
of marital happiness.*

Since nearly all of us have experienced divorce among our close friends or relatives, we have come to realize that divorce is not a cure for difficulty, but is merely an escape, and a weak one. We have come to realize also that the mere performance of a ceremony does not bring happiness and a successful marriage. Happiness does not come by pressing a button, as does the electric light; happiness is a state of mind and comes from within. It must be earned. It cannot be purchased with money; it cannot be taken for nothing.

Some think of happiness as a glamorous life of ease, luxury, and constant thrills; but true marriage is based on a happiness that is more than that, one that comes from giving, serving, sharing, sacrificing, and selflessness.

Two people coming from different backgrounds soon learn after the ceremony is performed that stark reality must be faced. There is no longer a life of fantasy or of make-believe; we must come out of the clouds and put our feet firmly on the earth.

Responsibility must be assumed and new duties must be accepted. Some personal freedoms must be relinquished and many adjustments, unselfish adjustments, must be made.

One comes to realize very soon after marriage that the spouse has weaknesses not previously revealed or discovered. The virtues that were constantly magnified during courtship now grow relatively smaller, and the weaknesses that seemed so small and insignificant during courtship now grow to sizeable proportions. The hour has come for understanding hearts, for self-appraisal, and for good common sense, reasoning, and planning. The habits of years now show themselves; the spouse may be stingy or prodigal, lazy or industrious, devout or irreligious, kind and cooperative or petulant and cross, demanding or giving, egotistical or self-effacing. The in-law problem comes closer into focus and the relationship of the spouses to in-laws is again magnified.

Often there is an unwillingness to settle down and assume the heavy responsibilities that immediately are there. Economy is reluctant to replace lavish living, and the young people seem often too eager "to keep up with the Joneses." There is often an unwillingness to make the necessary financial adjustments. Young wives often demand that all the luxuries formerly enjoyed in the prosperous homes of their successful fathers be continued in their own homes. Some of them are quite willing to help earn that lavish living by continuing employment after marriage. They consequently leave the home, where their duty lies, to pursue professional or business pursuits, thus establishing an economy that becomes stabilized so that it becomes very difficult to yield toward the normal family life. With both spouses working, competition rather than cooperation enters the family. Two weary workers return home with taut nerves, individual pride, and increased independence, and then misunderstandings arise. Little frictions pyramid into monumental ones. Frequently, spouses sinfully turn to old romances or take up new ones, and finally the seemingly inevitable break comes with a divorce, with its heartaches, bitterness, disillusionment, and always scars.

While marriage is difficult, and discordant and frustrated marriages are common, yet real, lasting happiness is possible, and marriage can be more an exultant ecstasy than the human mind can conceive. This is within the reach of every couple, every person. "Soulmates" are fiction and an illusion; and while every young man and young woman will seek with all diligence and prayerfulness to find a mate with whom life can be most compatible and beautiful, yet it is certain that almost any good man and good woman can have happiness and a successful marriage if both are willing to pay the price.

There is a never-failing formula that will guarantee to every couple a happy and eternal marriage; but like all formulas, the principle ingredients must not be left out, reduced, nor limited. The selection before courting and then the continued courting after the marriage process are equally important, but not more important than the marriage itself, the success of which depends upon the two individuals—not upon one, but upon two.

When a couple have commenced a marriage based upon reasonable standards, no combination of power can destroy that marriage except the power within either or both of the spouses themselves; and they must assume the responsibility generally. Other people and agencies may influence for good or bad; financial, social, political,

Happiness does not come by pressing a button,
as does the electric light; happiness is a state of mind and
comes from within.
It must be earned. It cannot be purchased
with money; it cannot be taken for nothing.

and other situations may seem to have a bearing. But the marriage depends first and always on the two spouses, who can always make their marriage successful and happy if they are determined, unselfish, and righteous.

The formula is simple; the ingredients are few, though there are many amplifications of each.

First, there must be the proper approach toward marriage, which contemplates the selection of a spouse who reaches as nearly as possible the pinnacle of perfection in all the matters that are of importance to the individuals. Then those two parties must come to the altar in the temple realizing that they must work hard toward this successful joint living.

Second, there must be great unselfishness, forgetting self and directing all of the family life and all pertaining thereunto to the good of the family, and subjugating self.

Third, there must be continued courting and expressions of affection, kindness, and consideration to keep love alive and growing.

Fourth, there must be complete living of the commandments of the Lord as defined in the gospel of Jesus Christ.

With these ingredients properly mixed and continually kept functioning, it is quite impossible for unhappiness to come, for misunderstandings to continue, or for breaks to occur. Divorce attorneys would need to transfer to other fields and divorce courts would be padlocked.

Two individuals approaching the marriage altar must realize that in order for them to attain the happy marriage they hope for, they must know that marriage is not a legal cover-all. Rather, it means sacrifice, sharing, and even a reduction of some personal liberties. It means long, hard economizing. It means children who bring with them financial burdens, service burdens, care and worry burdens; but also it means the deepest and sweetest emotions of all.

Before marriage, each individual is quite free to go and come as he pleases; to organize and plan his life as it seems best; to make all decisions with self as the central point. Sweethearts should realize before they take the vows that each must accept literally and fully that the good of the new little family must always be superior to the good of either spouse. Each party must eliminate the "I" and the "my" and substitute therefor "we" and "our." Every decision must take into consideration that now two or more are affected by it. As she approaches major decisions now, the wife will be concerned as to the effect they will have upon the parents, the children, the home, and their spiritual lives. The husband's choice of occupation, his social life, his friends, his every interest must now be considered in the light that he is only a part of a family, that the totalness of the group must be considered.

Every divorce is the result of selfishness on the part of one or the other or both parties to a marriage contract. Someone is thinking of self-comforts, conveniences, freedoms, luxuries, or ease. Sometimes the ceaseless pinpricking of an unhappy, discontented, and selfish spouse can finally add up to a serious physical violence. Sometimes people are goaded to the point where they erringly feel justified in doing the things that are so wrong. Nothing, of course, justifies sin.

Sometimes the husband or the wife feels neglected, mistreated, and ignored until he or she wrongly feels justified in adding to errors. If each spouse submits to frequent self-analysis and measures his own imperfections by the yardstick of perfection and the Golden Rule, and if each spouse sets about to correct self in every deviation found by such analysis rather than to set about to correct the deviations in the other party, then transformation comes and happiness is the result. There are many pharisaic people who marry who should memorize the parable of the Savior in Luke—people who prate their own virtues and pile up their own qualities of goodness and put them on the scales against the weaknesses of the spouse. They say, "I fast twice a week; I give tithes of all I possess." (See Luke 18:9-14.)

For every friction, there is a cause; and whenever there is unhappiness, each should search self to find the cause or at least that portion of the cause which originated in that self.

A marriage may not always be even and incident-less, but it can be one of great peace. A couple may have poverty, illness, disappointment, failures, and even death in the family, but even these will not rob them of their peace. The marriage can be successful so long as selfishness does not enter in. Troubles and problems will draw parents together into unbreakable unions if there is total unselfishness there. During the depression of the 1930s there was a definite drop in divorce. Poverty, failures, disappointment—they tied parents together. Adversity can cement relationships that prosperity can destroy.

The marriage that is based upon selfishness is almost certain to fail. The one who marries for wealth or the one who marries for prestige or social plane is certain to be disappointed. The one who marries to satisfy vanity and pride or who marries to spite or to show up another person is fooling only himself. But the one who marries to give happiness as well as receive it, to give service as well as to receive it, and looks after the interests of the two and then the family as it comes will have a good chance that the marriage will be a happy one.

There are many people who do not find divorce attorneys and who do not end their marriages, but who have permitted their marriage to grow stale and weak and cheap. There are spouses who have fallen from the throne of adoration and worship

Some think of happiness as a glamorous life of ease, luxury, and
constant thrills; but true marriage is based
on a happiness that is more than that,
one that comes from giving,
serving, sharing, sacrificing, and selflessness.

and are in the low state of mere joint occu-
pancy of the home, joint sitters at the ta-
ble, joint possessors of certain things that
cannot be easily divided. These people are
on the path that leads to trouble. These
people will do well to reevaluate, to renew
their courting, to express their affection, to
acknowledge kindnesses, and to increase
their consideration so their marriage can
again become beautiful, sweet, and growing.

Love is like a flower, and, like the body,
it needs constant feeding. The mortal
body would soon be emaciated and
die if there were not frequent feedings.
The tender flower would wither and die
without food and water. And so love, also,
cannot be expected to last forever unless it
is continually fed with portions of love,
the manifestation of esteem and admiration, the expressions of gratitude, and the
consideration of unselfishness.

Total unselfishness is sure to accom-
plish another factor in successful marriage.
If each spouse is forever seeking the interests, comforts, and happiness of the other,
the love found in courtship and cemented
in marriage will grow into mighty proportions. Many couples permit their marriages

to become stale and their love to grow cold like old bread or worn-out jokes or cold gravy. Certainly the foods most vital for love are consideration, kindness, thoughtfulness, concern, expressions of affection, embraces of appreciation, admiration, pride, companionship, confidence, faith, partnership, equality, and dependence.

To be really happy in marriage, there must be a continued faithful observance of the commandments of the Lord. No one, single or married, was ever sublimely happy unless he was righteous. There are temporary satisfactions and camouflaged situations for the moment, but permanent, total happiness can come only through cleanliness and worthiness. One who has a pattern of religious life with deep religious convictions can never be happy in an inactive life. The conscience will continue to afflict unless it has been seared, in which case the marriage is already in jeopardy. A stinging conscience can make life most unbearable. Inactivity is destructive to marriage, especially where the parties are inactive in varying degrees. Religious differences are the most trying and among the most unsolvable of all differences.

Marriage is ordained of God. It is not

*Every divorce is the result of selfishness on the part of one or the
other or both parties to a marriage contract.
Someone is thinking of self-comforts, conveniences,
freedoms, luxuries, or ease.
Sometimes the ceaseless pinpricking
of an unhappy, discontented, and selfish spouse
can finally add up to serious physical violence.
Sometimes people are goaded to the point where they erringly
feel justified in doing the things
that are so wrong.
Nothing, of course, justifies sin.*

merely a social custom. Without proper and successful marriage, one will never be exalted. Read the words of the Lord, that it is right and proper to be married.

This being true, the thoughtful, intelligent Latter-day Saint will plan his life carefully to be sure there are no impediments placed in the way. To make one serious mistake, one may place in the way obstacles that may never be removed and that may block the way to eternal life and godhood—our ultimate destiny. If two people love the Lord more than their own lives and then love each other more than their own lives, working together in total harmony with the gospel program as their basic structure, they are sure to have this great happiness. When a husband and wife go together frequently to the holy temple, kneel in prayer together in their home with their family, go hand in hand to their religious meetings, keep their lives wholly chaste, mentally and physically, so that their whole thoughts and desires and love are all centered in one being, their companion, and both are working together for the upbuilding of the kingdom of God, then happiness is at its pinnacle.

Sometimes in marriage there are other

cleavings, in spite of the fact that the Lord said, "Thou shalt love thy wife with all thy heart, and shalt cleave unto her and none else." (D&C 42:22.)

This means just as completely that "thou shalt love thy *husband* with all thy heart and shall cleave unto *him* and none else." Frequently, people continue to cleave unto their mothers and their fathers and their friends. Sometimes mothers will not relinquish the hold they have had upon their children, and husbands as well as wives return to their mothers and fathers for advice and counsel and to confide; whereas cleaving should be to the wife or husband in most things, and all intimacies should be kept in great secrecy and privacy from others.

A couple do well to immediately find their own home, separate and apart from those of the in-laws on either side. The home may be very modest and unpretentious, but still it is an independent domicile. Their married life should become independent of her folks and his folks. The couple love their parents more than ever; they cherish their counsel; they appreciate their association; but they must live their own lives, being governed by their own decisions, by their own prayerful considerations after they have received the counsel from those who should give it. To cleave does not mean merely to occupy the same home; it means to adhere closely, to stick together.

"Wherefore, it is lawful that . . . they twain shall be one flesh, and all this that the earth might answer the end of its creation;

"And that it might be filled with the measure of man, according to his creation before the world was made." (D&C 49:16-17.)

Our own record is not pleasing. Of 31,037 recent marriages, our records say only 14,169 were in the temple for eternity. This is 46 percent. There were 7,556 members married out of the Church. This is terribly disturbing to us. This is 24 percent, which means that about 9,000, or 30 percent, apparently thought so little of themselves and their posterity that they married out of the temple, which could give them a key to eternal life. Is it possible they do not know or do not care?

Of course, most such people who marry out of the Church and temple do not weigh the matter sufficiently. The survey I mentioned disclosed the fact that only about one out of seven would be converted and baptized into the Church. This is a great loss. It means that in many cases there is not only loss of the unbaptized spouse, but also of the children and even sometimes the other spouse.

We love those few who join the Church after marriage. We praise them and honor them, but the odds are against this happening. According to the figures given above, this means that nearly 6,500 of the new marriages may never find both parties finally joining the Church to make the family totally united. This grieves us very much. The total program of the Lord for the family cannot be enjoyed fully if the people are unequally yoked in marriage.

We call upon all youth to make such a serious, strong resolution to have a temple marriage that their determination will provide for them the rich promises of eternal marriage with its accompanying joys and happiness. This would please the Lord, who counts on each of us so heavily. He has said that eternal life can be had only in the way he has planned it.

"And a white stone is given to each of

those who come into the celestial kingdom, whereon is a new name written,
which no man knoweth save he that receiveth it. The new name is the key word."
(D&C 130:11.)

It is the *normal* thing to marry. It was
arranged by God in the beginning. One is
not wholly normal who does not want to
be married. Remember, ". . . neither is the
man without the woman, neither the
woman without the man, in the Lord." (1
Corinthians 11:11.)

No one can reject this covenant of celestial marriage and reach the eternal
kingdom of God. This is certain.

"In the celestial glory there are three
heavens or degrees;

"And in order to obtain the highest, a
man must enter into this order of the
priesthood [meaning the new and everlasting covenant of marriage];

"And if he does not, he cannot obtain
it.

"He may enter into the other, but that
is the end of his kingdom. . . ." (D&C
131:1-4.)

"For behold, I reveal unto you a new
and everlasting covenant; and if ye abide
not that covenant, then are ye damned.

. . ." (D&C 132:4.) And damned means stopped in progress.

These are the words of the Lord. They were said directly to us. There is no question about them.

"And as pertaining to the new and everlasting covenant, it was instituted for the fulness of my glory; and he that receiveth a fulness thereof must and shall abide the law. . . .

"Therefore, when they are out of the world [after they have died] they neither marry nor are given in marriage; but are appointed angels in heaven; which angels are ministering servants, to minister for those who are worthy of a far more, and an exceeding, and an eternal weight of glory.

"For these angels did not abide my law; therefore, they cannot be enlarged, but remain separately and singly, without exaltation, in their saved condition, to all eternity; and from henceforth are not gods, but are angels of God forever and ever.

"Abraham received all things, whatsoever he received, by revelation and commandment, by my word, saith the Lord, and hath entered into his exaltation and sitteth upon his throne.

"Go ye, therefore, and do the works of Abraham; enter ye into my law and ye shall be saved." (D&C 132:6, 16-17, 29, 32.)

This is the word of the Lord. It is very, very serious, and there is nobody who should argue with the Lord. He made the earth; he made the people. He knows the conditions. He set the program, and we are not intelligent enough or smart enough to be able to argue him out of these important things. He knows what is right and true.

We ask each Latter-day Saint to think of these things. Be sure that your marriage is right. Be sure that your life is right. Be sure that your part of the marriage is carried forward properly.

Now I ask the Lord to bless you. These things worry us considerably because there are too many divorces and they are increasing. It has come to be a common thing to talk about divorce. The minute there is a little crisis or a little argument in the family, we talk about divorce, and we rush to see an attorney. This is not the way of the Lord. We should go back and adjust our problems and make our marriage compatible and sweet and blessed.

I pray the Lord will bless each one who faces decisions before marriage and after marriage. I ask his blessings upon each one of you and give you my testimony that this church is true and divine, in the name of Jesus Christ. Amen.

Photography by
Brian K. Kelly
Kim Despain
Royce Bair
Kenneth Willes
Scott Beck
Spencer Dieber